EAT SMART

MEAT AND PROTEIN

Louise Spilsbury

Heinemann
LIBRARY

www.heinemann.co.uk/library
Visit our website to find out more information about Heinemann Library books.

To order:

 Phone 44 (0) 1865 888066

 Send a fax to 44 (0) 1865 314091

 Visit the Heinemann Bookshop at www.heinemann.co.uk/library to browse our catalogue and order online.

Heinemann Library is an imprint of Capstone Global Library Limited, a company incorporated in England and Wales having its registered office at 7 Pilgrim Street, London, EC4V 6LB – Registered company number: 6695582

"Heinemann" is a registered trademark of Pearson Education Limited, under licence to Capstone Global Library Limited

Text © Capstone Global Library Limited 2009
First published in hardback in 2009
The moral rights of the proprietor have been asserted.

Edited by Charlotte Guillain and Diyan Leake
Designed by Richard Parker and Manhattan Design
Picture research by Hannah Taylor
Production by Alison Parsons
Originated by Dot Gradations Ltd
Printed and bound in China by CTPS

ISBN 978 0 431066 18 9 (hardback)
13 12 11 10 09
10 9 8 7 6 5 4 3 2 1

British Library Cataloguing in Publication Data
Spilsbury, Louise
  Meat and protein. - (Eat smart)
  641.3'6

A full catalogue record for this book is available from the British Library.

Acknowledgements
We would like to thank the following for permission to reproduce photographs: © Alamy pp. **6** (Andrew Butterton), **10** (Nick Ayliffe), **12** (allOver photography), **17** (Jaubert Bernard); © DK Images p. **15**; © Getty Images p. **22** (Dorling Kindersley); © iStockphoto pp. **1**–**32** background images; © Pearson Education Ltd/MM Studios pp. **18**, **20**, **21**, **24**, **25** top, **25** bottom, **26**, **27** top, **27** bottom, **28**, **29** top, **29** bottom; © Photolibrary pp. **5** (Hemis), **7** (Foodpix), **8** (AlaskaStock), **14** (Pixland), **16** (Blend/Tanya Constantine), **19** (W. Reavill); © Rex Features pp. **9** (Martin Lee), **11** (Sabah Arar); © Science Photo Library p. **13** (Susumu Nishinaga); © StockFood UK p. **4** (Caroline Martin).

Cover photograph of reproduced with permission of © Photolibrary (Fancy).

CONTENTS

Some words are shown in bold, **like this**. You can find out what they mean by looking in the glossary.

WHAT IS PROTEIN?

Protein is a **nutrient** found in the food that you eat. Nutrients are substances that the body needs to function and stay healthy. Proteins are vital nutrients because they provide the body with the raw materials it needs to grow, to heal injuries, and to stay well. People get protein from animal and plant sources.

Animal sources

Meat from farm animals, including beef, pork, or chicken, is a major source of protein. People may eat cooked fresh meat or meat **processed** into foods such as burgers and sausages. Eggs and **dairy** products, such as milk and cheese, also contain protein. Farm animals supply over three-quarters of all animal protein. Fish and other seafood such as trout, haddock, and prawns are the major source of protein for over one billion people worldwide.

People may eat protein in the form of pieces of meat like this chop.

Nuts such as almonds are good sources of plant protein.

Plant proteins

Fruits and vegetables, from lettuce and carrots to tomatoes and pears, contain many useful nutrients, but very little protein. The only plant parts that contain significant proportions of protein are seeds. Seeds rich in protein include sunflower and pumpkin seeds, nuts such as walnuts, and **pulses**, including beans and lentils. Pulses grow in **pods** on plants in the bean family.

Burger beginnings

The hamburger got its name when German people from Hamburg, Germany, settled in the United States in the 1850s and introduced their recipes for ground beef patties. This way of eating meat proved so popular that Americans started to serve the hamburgers inside a bun as a quick snack and the fast food burger industry was born.

WHERE DO PROTEINS COME FROM?

The many different **proteins** that people eat come from a wide variety of animal and plant sources. Most are reared or grown on farms but some come from the wild.

Where does meat come from?

In the past, people used to hunt wild animals to eat. Today, most meat comes from farm animals such as cows and sheep. **Livestock** like these eat mostly plants, from grass and hay to corn and other grains. Plants use sunlight to make some of their own nutrients in their leaves. They take in other nutrients through their roots. Plant-eating animals take in some of these nutrients when they eat the plants.

Some livestock roam free in fields, but others live in crowded conditions inside factory farms.

Different kinds of meat

Most of the meat we eat comes from just a few types of animals. Chicken is the most widely eaten meat in the world, followed by beef from cows and pork and ham from pigs. Mutton (sheep meat) and goat meat are also popular. People eat smaller amounts of meats from other animals, such as kangaroo, rabbit, and venison (deer meat).

Preserving meat

People usually eat fresh meat which they buy from butchers in shops or markets. However, fresh meat does not keep for long before **bacteria** grow on it and make it unsafe to eat. In the past, people tried different ways of preserving meat, such as smoking, salting, or drying it, so they could transport it with them for a future meal. Today, most people buy meat that has been preserved by freezing or canning.

Before the widespread use of fridges and freezers, drying, salting, or smoking were the main methods of storing meat. Today, some people still use these methods because they create a distinctive flavour.

Making choices

The followers of some religions do not eat certain kinds of meat. For example, Muslims and Jews do not eat pork and most Hindus do not eat beef. Some people choose not to eat meat for other reasons. **Vegetarians** eat no meat or fish. Vegans are vegetarians who also eat no dairy products or eggs.

Where do fish come from?

Wild ocean fish such as sardines and tuna are caught on trawler boats. Trawlers may stay at sea for weeks at a time and use special equipment to locate and catch fish. Fish are often frozen onboard to keep them fresh until the boat returns to port.

Trawler boats use nets to sift though the water and catch fish.

Fish farmers raise fish such as trout and carp in ponds or pools. Some fish is **processed** before it is sold. It may have the skin and bones removed to make it easier to eat. In factories it may be made into a variety of fish products from fish soup to fish fingers.

White and oily fish

The fish people eat can be divided into white fish and oily fish.

White fish, such as cod, haddock, and whiting, store their reserve **fat** as oils in the **liver**. Oily fish, such as sardines, herring, mackerel, trout, and salmon, have oils throughout their body.

Oily fish is especially nutritious because it contains a special type of fat called **omega-3 fatty acids**. Omega 3 is excellent for the health of a person's nerves, eyes, and brain, and it helps maintain a healthy heart. A single portion per week supplies the amount you need. White fish contains some omega 3, but at much lower levels than oily fish.

Fish you eat with the bones in, such as whitebait, canned sardines and pilchards, are rich in calcium and phosphorous. The body uses these **minerals** to help make bones stronger.

Brainy fish?

For years, people have said that fish is brain food, without really knowing why. Now scientists believe that the omega-3 fatty acids in oily fish are particularly good for the development and function of the brain, because the brain is partly made up of these fats. So, eating a portion of oily fish such as salmon, tuna, or mackerel every week should boost your brain power as well as improve your health.

Seeds

Plants grow seeds to reproduce and the seeds may develop into new plants. Seeds contain everything a new plant needs to start growing, including nutrients such as protein. Seeds also contain other nutrients we can use, such as **vitamins** and **carbohydrates**.

Seeds come in many shapes and sizes and from different plants. Flax and poppy seeds come from colourful flowers. Pumpkin seeds come from inside pumpkins, which are large relatives of squashes. **Pulses** and nuts are seeds that come from particular types of plants.

Sunflower seeds grow in the centre of the flower head. The seeds are pressed to release oil, which is then used to make margarine and other foods.

Small but powerful!

Sesame seeds are among the smallest seeds we eat but are packed with protein and other nutrients such as minerals. Paintings in ancient Egyptian tombs dating back 4,000 years show bakers sprinkling sesame seeds into bread dough.

What are pulses?

Pulses are types of seeds from plants in the legume family, which includes pea and bean plants. These plants produce long seed cases or **pods**, each with several **edible** seeds inside. In some cases, such as French beans, you can eat the pods as well as the seeds. The most common types of pulse are lentils, split peas, black-eyed peas, chickpeas, broad beans, kidney beans, and butter beans. Pulses generally contain a higher proportion of **fibre** and less fat than other types of seeds. Another type of pulse is a soybean.

Nuts

Most nuts are largish, hard-shelled seeds that grow on trees. They range from coconuts and chestnuts to macadamias and hazelnuts. People always remove the shell before eating or cooking the softer **kernel** within. Nuts contain more fat or oil than many other seeds, but also lots of vitamins and minerals. The fat in nuts is also considered to be a healthier type of fat than that which is found in animal products.

◀ Pulses such as chickpeas are important protein for poorer people in many countries as they are cheaper to buy and more filling than meat.

WHY ARE PROTEINS GOOD FOR YOU?

People need **protein** to build a healthy body. Some proteins form body parts such as the bones, muscles, skin, and blood. Other proteins are building blocks for **enzymes** and **hormones**. Enzymes are important in breaking food down into **nutrients** in the digestive system. Hormones are chemical messengers that affect the function of **cells** around the body. Proteins also provide the body with **energy**.

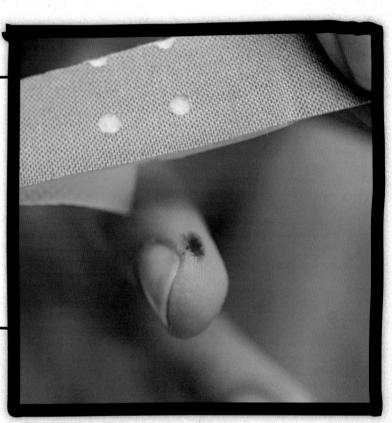

The skin and **tissues** beneath the skin's surface are made of protein, so the body needs adequate amounts of protein to repair them when they are damaged.

Protein protector

The body also uses protein to make **antibodies**. Antibodies are part of the **immune system**. They recognize and fight off **bacteria**, **viruses**, and other substances that cause infections or disease. These get into the body through the food people eat, the air they breathe, or through open cuts or sores. Proteins also act to help heal the wounds when people cut themselves.

Protein problems

A diet containing too little protein leaves people feeling tired and lacking in energy, and they may lose weight. The body may not produce enough antibodies to defend itself against infection and disease, and wounds may not heal. If children do not get enough protein, they cannot grow properly.

Too much protein is also unhealthy. Many protein-rich foods are high in fat. Too much fat in your diet can make you overweight and unhealthy. For example, fat can make your heart work less well.

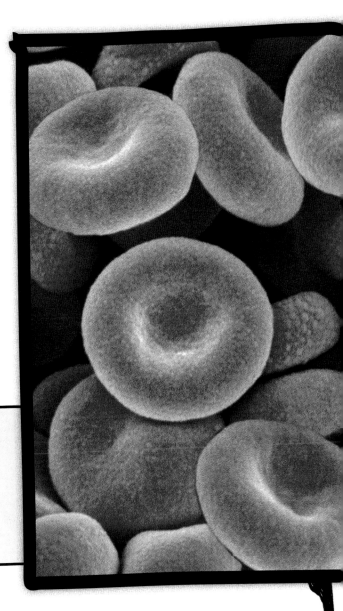

Red blood cells are made of a protein called haemoglobin. Haemoglobin transports **oxygen** from the lungs to all parts of the body.

Protein at work

Muscles in your arms and legs allow you to move around. The muscles are made of bundles of long strands of fibre built from proteins. The strands in arm muscles slide past each other when you want to bend your arm. This makes the muscles shorter and thicker, which pulls the arm bones towards each other.

Constructing proteins

Protein is made up of a long chain of **amino acids**. When you **digest** protein, your body breaks it down into the different amino acids. The body then strings the amino acids back together to form the particular proteins it needs. Amino acids can link together in many combinations to form different proteins. For example, the heart and lungs are made up of the same amino acids, but the amino acids combine in different ways to form the different organs (body parts).

Amino acids are a bit like beads on a necklace. You can use the same sort of beads to make different necklaces by changing the order and arrangement of the beads. In the body, the same kinds of amino acids are combined in different ways to make different body parts.

Eggs are sometimes called the perfect protein because they contain a small amount of all essential amino acids.

Which amino acids are essential?

There are two kinds of amino acids. One group is known as non-essential amino acids because the **liver** makes these from substances already inside the body. The other group is known as essential amino acids because the body cannot make them itself. You have to get these amino acids from the food you eat.

Animal protein from meat, fish, dairy foods, and eggs contains all of the essential amino acids. That is why meat proteins are sometimes called "complete proteins". Most plant proteins, such as those in many **pulses** and leafy vegetables, are "incomplete proteins", as they are missing one or two essential amino acids. However, plant foods also supply lots of healthy fibre, vitamins, and minerals.

Mix it up

If you eat two incomplete proteins together, often you will have all the amino acids that make up a complete protein. For example, peanut butter is missing an essential amino acid called methionine, and bread is lacking an essential amino acid called lysine. But when you make a peanut butter sandwich, you have a complete protein.

Vegetarians and protein

Apart from a few foods such as tofu from soybeans and some grains such as quinoa, most plant proteins are missing at least one essential amino acid. **Vegetarians** get all the essential amino acids they need by eating a range of plant and other foods, such as some cereals or grains, a mixture of pulses, nuts, and seeds, and some milk, cheese, eggs, or soya products. The important thing to remember is that the body cannot store protein, so everyone must eat some every day.

People in many cultures of the world do not eat meat, yet they have enough protein in their diet.

Other nutrients found in protein foods

Meat, poultry, fish, beans and peas, eggs, nuts, and seeds supply many other nutrients besides protein. These include B vitamins, vitamin E, and the minerals iron, zinc, and magnesium.

B vitamins from proteins help the body release energy, play an important role in making the **nervous system** work properly, help red blood cells to form, and help to build tissues. Vitamin E helps maintain healthy cells and provides protection against diseases such as cancer.

The body uses the mineral iron to carry oxygen in the blood. Magnesium is used in building bones and in releasing energy from muscles. Zinc is vital for keeping many of the body's systems working well, including the immune system.

Yogurt is a complete protein made from milk that is curdled by healthy bacteria. It also aids digestion and contains useful vitamins.

Don't sunbathe, eat fish and eggs instead

Oily fish and egg yolks are excellent sources of vitamin D as well as other nutrients. The body needs vitamin D to be able to use calcium and phosphorus, two minerals that are necessary for healthy bones. In the past, doctors advised people to get vitamin D from sitting in the sun, but now they know that too much sun can cause skin cancer, so they suggest people get vitamin D from their diet instead.

WHAT IS THE BEST WAY TO EAT PROTEIN FOODS?

Make sure you wash your hands, knife, and chopping board after handling meat so you do not transfer **bacteria** to other foods.

The best way to eat **protein**-rich foods is to eat them when they are fresh, to use healthy cooking methods to prepare them, and to have moderately sized portions.

Eating meat and fish

Some types of meat, especially red meat such as beef and pork, may contain lots of fat. Too much fat can make you overweight, which is unhealthy, so choose leaner, or less fatty, cuts of meat such as top sirloin, pork loin, and ham. You can also reduce fat by trimming white fat off meat and taking the skin off chicken or other poultry before cooking it.

Fish is lower in fat than meat so choose fish more often for lunch or dinner, especially fish rich in **omega-3 fatty acids** such as salmon, trout, and herring.

Healthy cooking methods

The healthiest ways to cook meat and fish are by grilling, **poaching**, baking, or **steaming**. These cooking methods do not add fat to food, as frying does. However, stir-frying meat or fish in a hot pan with a small amount of oil is also a good way to cook. This ensures a short cooking time and seals in the flavour. Avoid adding buttery or high-fat sauces after cooking.

Grilling is a healthy method of preparing fish to eat because there is no need to add oil or butter to cook it.

Read the labels

Most **processed** meats such as hams, sausages, frankfurters, and luncheon or deli meats have added salt. Even some fresh meats may have been treated with a salt solution. Eating too much salt can cause high **blood pressure**, which can result in heart disease when you are older. So, reduce the amount of processed foods you eat and read the labels to check they do not contain too much added salt.

Eating eggs

You can cook and eat eggs on their own by boiling, poaching, or frying them. You can also use eggs as an ingredient in quiches, omelettes, and cakes. You should not eat raw eggs. Raw eggs may contain bacteria that could make you ill. Cooking eggs kills off these bacteria and makes the eggs safe to eat.

Buying and cooking pulses

Tinned **pulses** are ready to use, but you have to soak dried pulses in water and then cook them in boiling water first. Some dried pulses contain small amounts of unsafe chemicals called **toxins**, but boiling makes them safe. You can use cooked or tinned beans and pulses as a main dish or part of a meal. For example, you could eat split pea, lentil, or bean soup, baked beans, bean enchiladas, rice and beans, or try stirring cooled beans and lentils into salads.

 Lentils do not need to be soaked before use and they cook much more quickly than other dried pulses. You can add them straight to bubbling stews or sauces.

↑ The best way to cook seeds is by roasting them. This concentrates their natural flavour.

How to eat nuts and seeds

Whole nuts make a healthy snack, but choose those without added sugar and salt. You can also use nuts in place of meat. Try toasted peanuts or cashews in a vegetable stir fry, or walnuts or pecans with a green salad. You can bake flaked and ground nuts in flapjacks or muffins, or sprinkle them on top of frozen yogurt. Sunflower, pumpkin, and other seeds can be stirred into breakfast cereals and salads or added to toppings on bakes and crumbles.

Peanut butter: neither nut nor butter!

Peanuts are not nuts. They are pulses from the groundnut plant. The **pods** on this plant grow underground and each pod contains two nuts. People can make peanut butter by simply grinding peanuts. Peanut butter is so-called because, like butter, you can spread it on bread.

HOW MUCH PROTEIN SHOULD YOU EAT?

Protein is a very important part of a healthy diet and you should eat some protein foods every day. However, your body does not need as much protein as it does certain other types of food, such as fruit and vegetables.

There is a very wide range of sources of protein.

Portions of protein

You should eat a moderate amount of protein as part of a healthy, balanced diet. An easy way to get the balance right is to eat a small amount of protein with each of your three main meals, although some people may need more or less than this depending on their needs. Most people eat enough protein foods or even too much, so try to choose leaner cuts of meat and eat a more varied selection of protein foods, such as nuts or lentils in place of meat sometimes.

A balanced diet

A balanced diet contains a variety of foods that together provide all the nutrients people need to be healthy. The food plate diagram on the next page shows the types and proportions of foods needed for a well-balanced diet.

It shows how people should eat lots of fruit and vegetables, plenty of grains and other **starchy** carbohydrate foods such as bread, rice, pasta and potatoes, some milk and dairy foods, some proteins such as meat, fish, eggs, and beans, and just a small amount of foods and drinks that are high in fat or sugar.

Protein foods should make up about one-tenth of your overall diet.

Meat and protein recipes

Fish burgers

This is an easy recipe to help you eat more fish. It makes four fish burgers using fresh tuna or salmon.

Ingredients

- 550 g (1 lb 4 oz) salmon or tuna fillet (without bones or skin)
- 2 tablespoons Dijon mustard
- Salt and pepper
- 1 egg
- 1 tablespoon oats
- 2 tablespoons plain wholewheat flour
- 4 bread rolls
- Knob of unsalted butter
- 1 small soft lettuce
- 1 small red onion

Equipment

- Knife
- Bowl
- Large non-stick frying pan
- Fish slice

WHAT YOU DO

1 Use a knife to cut away any brown bits from the fillet and throw them away. Then finely chop the rest of the fish.

2 Put the fish pieces in a bowl. Add the mustard and a little salt and pepper, and stir. Crack the egg into a bowl and stir with a fork before adding to the fish mixture. Then add the oats.

Always ask an adult to help you in the kitchen.

EAT SMART

3 Divide the mixture into four even-sized portions. Then either damp your hands with a little water or rub them with a coating of flour before shaping the burgers. Add a little salt and pepper to the flour and use this to lightly coat the burgers.

4 Rub butter onto the base of a non-stick baking tray. Cook the burgers in an oven for 15–20 minutes, until they are browned and cooked through. Use a fish slice to flip them over after 10 minutes to ensure both sides are browned.

5 Cut the rolls in half and grill them if you like. Place the bottom of each roll on a plate. Place a burger on top of each roll. You could add a lettuce leaf and a sliced onion ring before putting the top of each roll on the burger.

Seed bars

Make these seed bars to take with you to school or to keep in the fridge for when you want a healthy snack. They should last about a fortnight in the fridge. This recipe should make about 16 bars.

WHAT YOU DO

Ingredients

- 400 g (14 oz) sesame seeds
- 400 g (14 oz) sunflower seeds
- 400 g (14 oz) coconut, flaked
- 400 g (14 oz) cashew nuts
- 350 g (12 oz) honey

Equipment

- Mixing bowl
- Wooden spoon
- Square baking tray
- Knife

1 Stir together all of the ingredients in a mixing bowl.

2 Pour the mixture into the baking tray and press it down with the back of a spoon.

Always ask an adult to help you in the kitchen.

3 Cover the baking tray with foil and put it into the fridge for a few hours until the seed mixture sets firm.

4 Cut the seed mixture into bars. Wrap each bar in cling film or foil and refrigerate until you want to eat it.

Chilli con carne

Chilli con carne is Spanish for "chilli with meat". This meat dish can be served with rice or with tortilla breads.

Ingredients

- 350 g (13 oz) minced beef
- 1 carrot
- 1 large onion
- 1 green pepper
- 1 red pepper
- 50 g (2 oz) mushrooms
- 1 teaspoon chilli powder
- Black pepper
- 400 g (14 oz) tin chopped tomatoes
- 400 g (14 oz) tin kidney beans
- 1 teaspoon tomato purée
- 1 clove garlic

Equipment

- Knife
- Chopping board
- Frying pan
- Wooden spoon
- Garlic crusher (optional)
- Colander

WHAT YOU DO

1 Prepare the vegetables first. Peel and slice the onion. Peel and finely chop the garlic, or crush it with a garlic crusher. Peel and chop the carrot into small dice. Wash and then cut the mushrooms, red pepper, and green pepper into thin slices. Put the vegetables into a bowl.

2 Cook the minced beef in a large saucepan over a medium-heat hob or gas ring for about 5 minutes, stirring all the time.

Always ask an adult to help you in the kitchen.

3 Add the vegetables, the chilli powder, and black pepper to the meat. Stir well and cook for a few minutes.

4 Add the tinned tomatoes and the tomato purée. Bring to the boil and simmer gently for about 30 minutes. Stir occasionally.

5 Drain the kidney beans in a colander and rinse them under cold water. Add the beans to the mince mixture. Cook for a further 5 minutes.

You can make a vegetarian version of this chilli. Instead of using meat, stir in 225 g (8 oz) of green lentils (cooked in simmering water) when you add the tinned tomatoes.

If you use dried kidney beans, you need to soak them in clean, cold water for at least 8 hours before cooking them. Then you must boil them for at least 10 minutes, before simmering them for at least 45 minutes to finish cooking them. Boiling kidney beans for 10 minutes is vital to make them safe to eat.

GLOSSARY

amino acid basic building block of proteins

antibody protein that the body makes to protect itself from substances such as bacteria that could harm it

bacteria extremely small organisms that can only be seen using a microscope. Some bacteria can cause disease or sickness.

blood pressure force exerted by the heart in pumping blood around the body

carbohydrate a type of nutrient we get from food. The body breaks carbohydrates down into sugars that it uses for energy.

cell all living things are made up of millions of microscopic parts called cells. Different parts of the body are made up of different types of cells.

dairy made from milk

digest the name for the way the stomach, intestine, and other body parts work together to break down food into pieces so small they dissolve in liquid and pass into the blood

edible safe to eat

energy people require energy to be active and to carry out all body processes including breathing

enzyme protein that speeds up chemical processes and reactions in the body. For example, the enzymes produced by the stomach help the body digest food.

fat one of the nutrients that give you energy. The body uses only a small amount of fat, so eating too much can make people overweight.

fibre part of food that cannot be digested but helps keep the bowels working regularly

hormone chemical substance that travels through the blood to organs and tissues, where it changes their function, structure, and behaviour

immune system the human body's system of defences against disease. The immune system includes white blood cells and antibodies that react against bacteria and other harmful substances.

kernel inner and usually edible part of a seed, grain, or nut

liver a body part located inside the body, below the chest. The liver cleans the blood and produces bile, a substance that helps break down food in the digestive system.

livestock animals raised on a farm for meat or milk such as cows or sheep

mineral substance that comes from non-living sources such as rocks that break down and become part of the soil. Some of the nutrients that plants take in through their roots are called minerals.

nervous system system of nerves that regulates and coordinates all the body's activities

nutrient substance found in food that is essential for life

omega-3 fatty acid a nutrient found in certain fish, plants, and nut oils. Omega-3 fatty acids are essential for health but cannot be made by the body, so we need to get them from food.

oxygen a gas in the air

poach cook food in simmering (gently boiling) water

pod dry fruit that consists of a long, two-sided case to hold a plant's seeds, such as the pea pod

processed prepared and changed from a natural state to make a new product, as when milk is processed into cheese or meat is processed into sausages

protein nutrient that provides the raw materials the body needs to grow and repair itself

pulse edible seed that grows inside the pods of various plants

starchy something containing starch. Starch is a plant's store of excess glucose (food).

steam cook in the steam that rises from a pan of boiling water

tissue group of similar cells that act together to perform a particular job. For example, skin cells form skin tissue.

toxin substance that is harmful to the body

vegetarian person who does not eat meat or fish

virus microorganism that can infect cells and cause disease

vitamin nutrient that people require to grow and stay healthy

FIND OUT MORE

At **www.eatwell.gov.uk** there is a wide range of information including tips on eating healthy foods and keeping food safe.

The BBC website **www.bbc.co.uk/health/healthy_living/nutrition** covers many aspects of healthy eating.

At **kidshealth.org/kid** there is a large section on staying healthy and some recipes to try.

Click on the 'Healthy eating' link at **www.nutrition.org.uk** for ideas for healthier lunches, a closer look at the Eatwell plate, and more.

INDEX